Introduction

I first came across the work of Panayiotis Kalorkoti at the Royal College of Art, London, in 1982, and it immediately struck a very odd chord. At the centre of *The Studio* , for instance, a top-hatted Goya is painting his *Maya*; to either side of his easel, ten other sitters, including a cardinal and a general, wait in line; but a shadowy bugaboo from the *Disporates* is also present on the dais, while behind, from enormous frames, twelve wild Rasputins (they are in fact "self-portraits") scream back at us. The literal sense might be to point up the absurdity of Goya's portrait-rôle, when contrasted with the artist's (Goya's, or Kalorkoti's) private vision. But these "self-portraits" are themselves a parody, whose cod-angst or mock-confession sets in question all authenticity.

Something of that comedy of displacement seems to me never far away from all Kalorkoti's subsequent imagery, even from the work collected here, where the artist takes on public responsibility. Frank Whitford in 1989 wrote of Kalorkoti's "grasp of reality", but emphasised his Cypriot origins (he was already nine years old when he first came to England) and his resultant sense of "a partly alien culture". To me, Kalorkoti's wonderfully firm graphic line manages simultaneously to convey both authority, and the open-eyed innocence of a stranded Martian.

In reproduction this line, and the areas of flat or patterned colour it encloses, can resemble the stencilled imagery of silkscreen, but in fact the medium is colour-etching which involves a much more complex process. Silkscreen had proved insufficiently deliberated, or substantial: "Although silkscreen has many positive qualities I feel that by nature it is too mechanical... In particular, I find the way the ink lies on the surface of the paper unattractive". It was as though he needed an extra layer; by first silkscreening the image onto the etching-plate, he was able to achieve a broken quality *within* the firm outline, just as the flat fields of colour become, through the biting of the acid, granular and variegated.

These fields of colour, which often need to generate space, and, as in *Let the Sky In* [8], carry big shifts of implied viewpoint, are very precisely judged: "Sometimes I'll spend several hours trying and retrying variations of a colour". And the final colour may emerge out of several layers, each needing to be printed with just the right pressure.

Used in this way, colour-etching approximates to the finality and elegance of a Japanese woodblock print. I am thinking, for example, of the close-up heads of *Suspicion* [21], where large spreading areas of blank flesh are eventually broken by very strongly pronounced features. It is as though the precision and restraint of a Holbein drawing was united with the fierce, emphatic, almost caricatural delineation of one of Sharaku's actor-prints.

As Kalorkoti explained when (for the first and only time) we met this year: "My work has an element of construction". I see him as a master of collage - of the juxtaposition of images, from different areas of reality, and often from different visual languages. Collage can be a wonderful way of imaging the structure of the mind, of how it processes and orders the most disparate experience; this possibility constantly renewed itself in Twentieth Century art right up to the "fragmentary epics" of R.B. Kitaj in the Sixties. But in recent years (perhaps because it became too much identified with 'pop' silkscreen and its often facile ironic disjunctions) collage has become rather lost to sight. It takes an artist with Panayiotis Kalorkoti's peculiar mixture of innocence and visual resource, of wit and seriousness, to show how collage can still serve to combine dream and reality, information and commentary to unique effect.

This "retrospective view" focuses exclusively on the project-based works made in the past six years. What it does not suggest, perhaps, is the more "subversive" aspects of Kalorkoti, whose carnival satire sometimes recalls Ensor and the popular themes of "the topsy-turvy world". All the same, it may be helpful to know that his catalogue for the National Garden Festival at Gateshead, after reproducing the prints included here [32-39] ends with a weird "drawings" section; twenty-five pages, with nine portrait heads on each, making a total of 225 mostly full-face delineations of all those involved in the project. Taken individually, many of those heads may have the humanity of Kalorkoti's full-scale prints - his portrait of the Director of the The Grizedale Society, Bill Grant, for example. But massed like this, this overwhelming assembly of *mugs* shades into his other "collections" - becoming indistinguishable from those schematic faces, those quasi-tribal masks, and those Grizedale ideograms, all those lists, which seem to be one method by which a Martian tries to understand our mysterious world.

Timothy Hyman

PANAYIOTIS KALORKOTI

A Retrospective View

1985-91

Design Works, Gateshead

2 June - 11 July 1992

 International

 COURTAULDS COATINGS

Foreword

The work of Panayiotis Kalorkoti in many ways complement the style of the Design Works building. His use of bright, primary colours, the hard-edged, linear graphics, the interaction between man and the environment and the collage of existing and created images reflect much of the visual aspects of Design Works.

Over the last year Design Works has hosted a number of significant exhibitions of Fine Art and Sculpture. Panayiotis Kalorkoti's retrospective view spanning a six year period is an important showing of 46 works, many of which are inspired by the North of England, its people, activities and environs.

Felling, Gateshead is not the sort of place you would expect to find an art gallery. Set in an urban landscape of industrial buildings, Design Works is itself a unique environment - a business centre for creative people and an exhibition and conference centre attracting a large number of visitors. The ground floor gallery, 5000 square feet of light and spacious floorspace lends itself to 2 and 3 dimensional works and is the main thoroughfare for the building.

Peter Rodger
Chief Executive

1. Chips with Everything

2. Untitled / Playhouse

3. The Ordered Condition

4. Golden Girls

5. Strength and Beauty

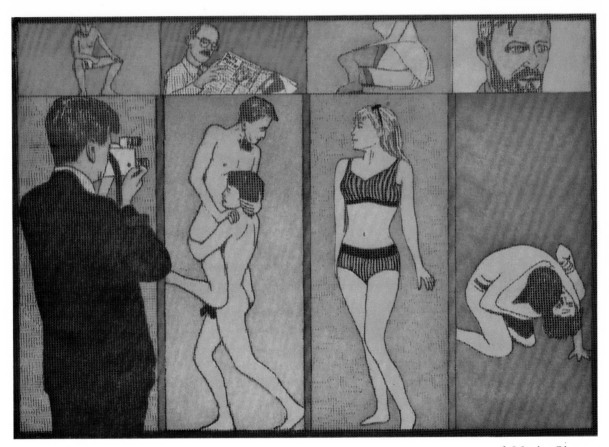

6. Moving Pictures

7. The Father

8. Let the Sky In

9. Mother and Daughter

10. Cast of Characters

11. Chips with Everything

12. Untitled / Playhouse

13. The Ordered Condition

14. Golden Girls

15. Strength and Beauty

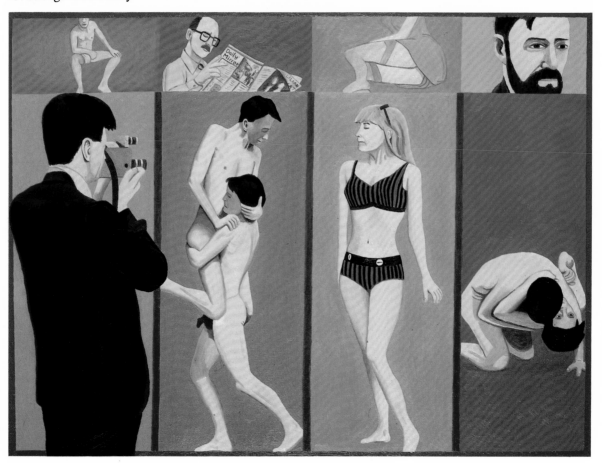

16. Moving Pictures

17. The Father

18. Let the Sky In

19. Mother and Daughter

20. Cast of Characters

21. Suspicion

22. The Letter

23. The Rivals

24. IWM Commission No. 1

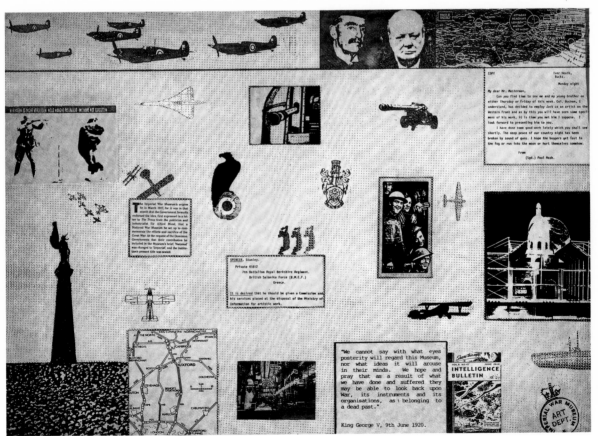

25. IWM Commission No. 2

26. Darlington 1

27. Darlington 2

28. Darlington 3

29. Darlington 4

30. Hartlepool 1

31. Hartlepool 2

32. Man with Cat

33. Woman with Cigarette

34. Working for the Landscape

35. Planning Meeting

36. Reflective Variations

37. Good News

38. Landmarks

39. Reconstruction

40. Grizedale 1

41. Grizedale 2

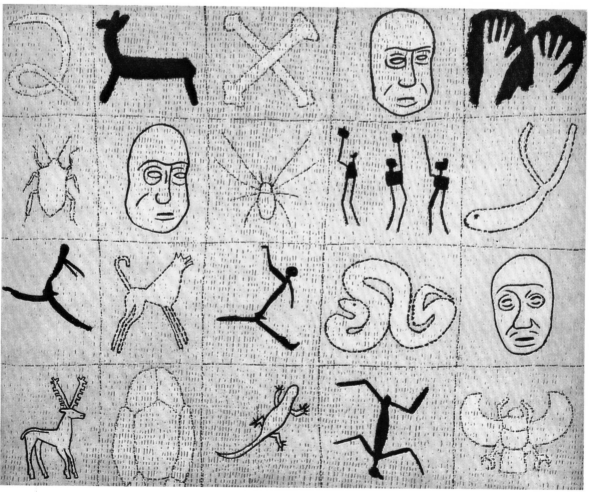

42. Grizedale 3

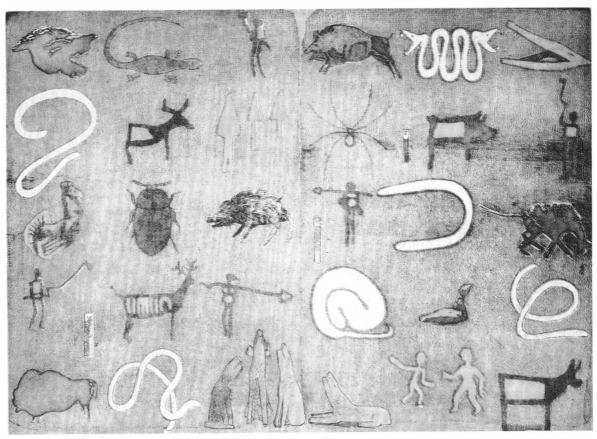

43. Grizedale 4

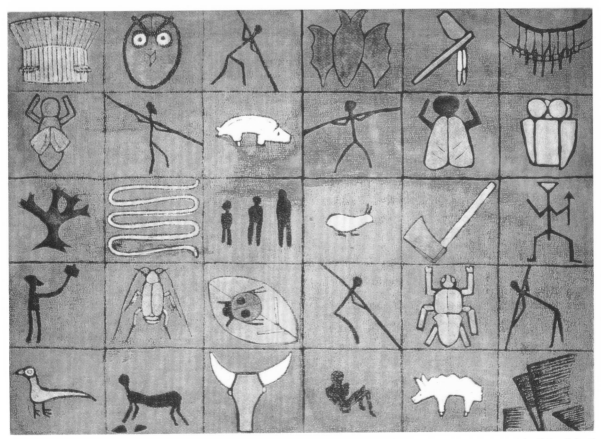

44. Grizedale 5

45. Grizedale 6

46. Grizedale 7

Catalogue

1. **Chips with Everything** 1985
Multi-Plate Etching 56.5 x 76.2cm
Edition of 50

2. **Untitled/Playhouse** 1985
Multi-Plate Etching 56.5 x 76.2cm
Edition of 50

3. **The Ordered Condition** 1985
Multi-Plate Etching 56.5x76.2cm
Edition of 50

4. **Golden Girls** 1985
Multi-Plate Etching 56.5x76.2cm
Edition of 50

5. **Strength and Beauty** 1985
Multi-Plate Etching 56.5x76.2cm
Edition of 50

6. **Moving Pictures** 1985
Multi-Plate Etching 56.5x76.2cm
Edition of 50

7. **The Father** 1985
Multi-Plate Etching 56.5x76.2cm
Edition of 50

8. **Let the Sky In** 1985
Multi-Plate Etching 56.5x76.2cm
Edition of 50

9. **Mother and Daughter** 1985
Etching 56.5x75.6cm
Edition of 30

10. **Cast of Characters** 1985
Etching 56.5x75.6cm
Edition of 30

11. **Chips with Everything** 1985-86
Oil on Canvas 52.7x72.7cm

12. **Untitled/Playhouse** 1985
Oil on Canvas 51.4x71.1cm

13. **The Ordered Condition** 1985-86
Oil on Canvas 52x71.1cm

14. **Golden Girls** 1985-86
Oil on Canvas 52x71.1cm

15. **Strength and Beauty** 1985
Oil on Canvas 51.4x69.2cm

16. **Moving Pictures** 1985-86
Oil on Canvas 52.7x71.7cm

17. **The Father** 1985
Oil on Canvas 52x71.1cm

18. **Let the Sky In** 1985
Oil on Canvas 52.7x70.5cm

19. **Mother and Daughter** 1985-86
Oil on Canvas 52.7x71.1cm

20. **Cast of Characters** 1986
Oil on Canvas 52.7x71.7cm

21. **Suspicion** 1988
Multi-Plate Etching 56.5x76.2cm
Edition of 10

22. **The Letter** 1988
Multi-Plate Etching 56.5x76.2cm
Edition of 10

23. **The Rivals** 1988
Multi-Plate Etching 56.5x76.2cm
Edition of 10

24. **Imperial War Museum Commission No.1** 1988
Multi-Plate Etching 56.5x76.2cm
Edition of 10

25. **Imperial War Museum Commission No.2** 1988
Multi-Plate Etching 56.5x76.2cm
Edition of 10

26. **Darlington 1** 1989
Multi-Plate Etching 56.x76.2cm
Edition of 10

27. **Darlington 2** 1989
Multi-Plate Etching 56.5x76.2cm
Edition of 10

28. **Darlington 3** 1989
Multi-Plate Etching 56.5x76.2cm
Edition of 10

29. **Darlington 4** 1989
Multi-Plate Etching 56.5x76.2cm
Edition of 10

30. **Hartlepool 1** 1989
Multi-Plate Etching 56.5x76.2cm
Edition of 10

31. **Hartlepool 2** 1989
Multi-Plate Etching 56.5x76.2cm
Edition of 10

32. **Man with Cat** 1989
Multi-Plate Etching 76.2x56.5cm
Edition of 10

33. **Woman with Cigarette** 1989
Multi-Plate Etching 76.2x56.5cm
Edition of 10

34. **Working for the Landscape** 1990
Multi-Plate Etching 56.5x76.2cm
Edition of 10

35. **Planning Meeting** 1990
Multi-Plate Etching 56.5x76.2cm
Edition of 10

36. **Reflective Variations** 1990
Multi-Plate Etching 56.5x76.2cm
Edition of 10

37. **Good News** 1990
Multi-Plate Etching 56.5x76.2cm
Edition of 10

38. **Landmarks** 1990
Multi-Plate Etching 56.5x76.2cm
Edition of 10

39. **Reconstruction** 1990
Multi-Plate Etching 56.5x76.2cm
Edition of 10

40. **Grizedale 1** 1989
Multi-Plate Etching 56.5x76.2cm
Edition of 10

41. **Grizedale 2** 1989
Multi-Plate Etching 56.5x76.2cm
Edition of 10

42. **Grizedale 3** 1989
Multi-Plate Etching 56.5x76.2cm
Edition of 10

43. **Grizedale 4** 1991
Multi-Plate Etching 56.5x76.2cm
Edition of 10

44. **Grizedale 5** 1991
Multi-Plate Etching 56.5x76.2cm
Edition of 10

45. **Grizedale 6** 1991
Multi-Plate Etching 56.5x76.2cm
Edition of 10

46. **Grizedale 7** 1991
Multi-Plate Etching 56.5x76.2cm
Edition of 10

Biography

Born in Cyprus 1957

1976-80 Newcastle upon Tyne University, B.A. (Hons.)
         1st Class in Fine Art

1982-85 Royal College of Art, London, M.A. in
         Printmaking.

1985   Artist in Residence at Leeds Playhouse

1986-87 Koninklijke Akademie voor Kunst en
         Vormgeving, 's-Hertogenbosch
         (Netherlands Government Scholarship)

1988   Bartlett Fellow in the Visual Arts
         (Newcastle upon Tyne University)

1992   Artist in Residence, Cleveland County

Taught part-time and visiting Lecturer at a number of Art
Schools

Commissions

1988   Imperial War Museum, London
         People's Theatre, Newcastle

1989   Borough of Darlington
         Borough of Hartlepool
         Grizedale Society (Theatre in the Forest)

1990   National Garden Festival, Gateshead

1991   Grizedale Society (Theatre in the Forest)

Public Collections

Stedelijk Museum, Amsterdam
British Council
Imperial War Museum
Laing Art Gallery, Newcastle
Northern Arts
IBM
Rank Xerox

Awards

1983   Granada Prize

1987   British Council

1988   A.B.S.A.
         Northern Arts

1990   A.B.S.A.

1991   Lowick House Bursary

Solo Exhibitions

1980   Newcastle Polytechnic Gallery

1981   Bede Gallery, Jarrow
Hendersons Gallery, Edinburgh

1982   Bede Monastery Museum, Jarrow
Ceolfrith Gallery, Sunderland Arts Centre
Pentonville Gallery, London

1984   Abbot Hall Gallery, Kendal

1987   The Minories, Colchester
Steendrukkerij Amerstam B.V.

1988-89   Hatton Gallery, Newcastle and tour: Darlington Arts Centre; Gray Art Gallery and Museum, Hartlepool; Queen's Hall Arts Centre, Hexham (Catalogue)

1990   Imperial War Museum, London (Catalogue)
National Garden Festival, Gateshead (Catalogue)

1992   Design Works, Gateshead (Catalogue)
Cleveland Gallery, Middlesbrough and tour: Steendrukkerij Amerstam B.V. (Catalogue)

Group Exhibitions

1980   The Stone Gallery, Newcastle

1981   'Small Works' Newcastle Polytechnic Gallery

1982   'and Printmaking' Waterloo Gallery, London (Catalogue)

1983   'Stowells Trophy' Royal Academy of Arts, London
'Northern Young Contemporaries' (awarded Granada Prize) Whitworth Art Gallery, Manchester

1984   Bath Festival Painting Competition
'New Contemporaries' ICA, London (Catalogue)

1985   'Printmakers at the Royal College of Art' Concourse Gallery, Barbican Centre, London (Catalogue)
'Fresh Air' St. Paul's Gallery, Leeds
'Whitworth Young Contemporaries' Whitworth Art Gallery, Manchester

1986   'Tradition and Innovation in Printmaking Today' Concourse Gallery, Barbican Centre, London and tour: Milton Keynes Exhibition Gallery; Ferens Art Gallery, Hull; Andrew Grant Gallery, Edinburgh; Aspex Gallery, Portsmouth (Catalogue)
'Between Identity and Politics, A New Art' Gimpel Fils, London and tour: Darlington Arts Centre; Gimpel and Weitzenhoffer, New York (Catalogue)
'Fresh Art' Concourse Gallery, Barbican Centre, London (Catalogue)
'Whitechapel Open' Whitechapel Art Gallery, London

1987   Athena Art Awards, Concourse Gallery, Barbican Centre, London
'Which Side of the Fence' Imperial War Museum, London

1989   'The Artistic Records Committee: A Retrospective 1972-1989' Imperial War Museum, London

1991   Museum of Modern Art, Oxford

ISBN 0 9519585 0 X

Published by Design Works (Gateshead) Limited
Copyright © Panayiotis Kalorkoti
Photography by Graham Oliver
Catalogue Design by Peter Morrill
Printed by Colden Offset Ltd.